READY, STEADY, PRACTISE!

Frances Naismith

Fractions & Decimals
Pupil Book Year 4

Features of this book

- Clear explanations and worked examples for each fractions and decimals topic from the KS2 National Curriculum.

- Questions split into three sections that become progressively more challenging:

Warm up

Test yourself

Challenge yourself

- 'How did you do?' checks at the end of each topic for self-evaluation.

- Regular progress tests to assess pupils' understanding and recap on their learning.

- Answers to every question in a pull-out section at the centre of the book.

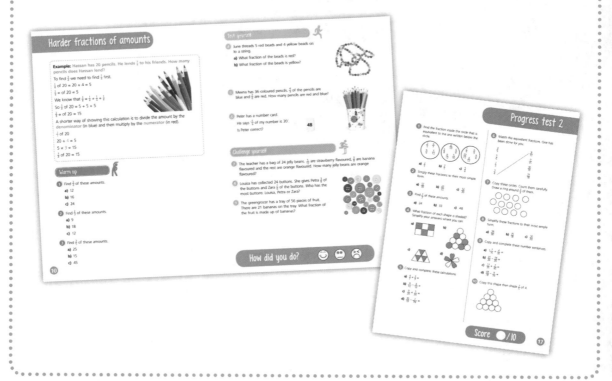

Contents

Equivalent fractions

Here are three shapes that are all the same size. The first one is divided into halves, the second into quarters and the third into eighths. Halves means two equal parts, quarters means four equal parts and eighths means eight equal parts.

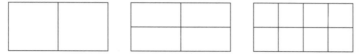

Some different parts of the shapes have been shaded.

By shading different parts, we can see that:

$$\frac{1}{2} = \frac{2}{4} = \frac{4}{8}$$

$$\frac{1}{4} = \frac{2}{8}$$

These are all equivalent fractions.

Look at the fraction wall below. How many other equivalent fractions can you find?

1											
$\frac{1}{2}$						$\frac{1}{2}$					
$\frac{1}{3}$				$\frac{1}{3}$				$\frac{1}{3}$			
$\frac{1}{4}$			$\frac{1}{4}$			$\frac{1}{4}$			$\frac{1}{4}$		
$\frac{1}{5}$		$\frac{1}{5}$		$\frac{1}{5}$		$\frac{1}{5}$		$\frac{1}{5}$			
$\frac{1}{6}$		$\frac{1}{6}$		$\frac{1}{6}$		$\frac{1}{6}$		$\frac{1}{6}$		$\frac{1}{6}$	
$\frac{1}{8}$	$\frac{1}{8}$	$\frac{1}{8}$	$\frac{1}{8}$	$\frac{1}{8}$	$\frac{1}{8}$	$\frac{1}{8}$	$\frac{1}{8}$				
$\frac{1}{10}$	$\frac{1}{10}$	$\frac{1}{10}$	$\frac{1}{10}$	$\frac{1}{10}$	$\frac{1}{10}$	$\frac{1}{10}$	$\frac{1}{10}$	$\frac{1}{10}$	$\frac{1}{10}$		
$\frac{1}{12}$	$\frac{1}{12}$	$\frac{1}{12}$	$\frac{1}{12}$	$\frac{1}{12}$	$\frac{1}{12}$	$\frac{1}{12}$	$\frac{1}{12}$	$\frac{1}{12}$	$\frac{1}{12}$	$\frac{1}{12}$	$\frac{1}{12}$

Warm up

1 Look at the shaded fractions of these shapes. Write the fraction that is shaded in each shape.

a)  b)   c)  d) 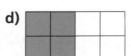 e)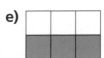

2 Using the fraction wall, find equivalent fractions for the following:

a) $\frac{1}{2}$

b) $\frac{1}{4}$

c) $\frac{3}{4}$

d) $\frac{1}{5}$

Test yourself

3 Look at the fraction pairs below. Write the bigger fraction from each pair.

a) $\frac{1}{5}$ $\frac{1}{8}$

b) $\frac{2}{10}$ $\frac{2}{12}$

c) $\frac{1}{4}$ $\frac{4}{12}$

4 Copy these fractions in order from the smallest to the largest.

$\frac{3}{4}$ $\frac{3}{8}$ $\frac{1}{4}$ $\frac{1}{2}$ $\frac{1}{6}$ $\frac{1}{5}$

Challenge yourself

5 Copy the fraction pairs. Use the symbols **>**, **<** or **=** to make each statement correct. Remember to make equivalent fractions.

a) $\frac{2}{3}$ ☐ $\frac{9}{12}$

b) $\frac{3}{8}$ ☐ $\frac{2}{4}$

c) $\frac{5}{10}$ ☐ $\frac{2}{5}$

6 Using the fraction wall on page 4 to help you, estimate how many $\frac{1}{24}$ths are equivalent to $\frac{1}{2}$.

How did you do?

Simplify fractions

To make fractions easier to work with we simplify them to their lowest or most simple form.

To simplify a fraction we look for a number that will divide into both the **numerator** and the **denominator**.

Example: Simplify $\frac{4}{12}$ to $\frac{1}{3}$

To simplify $\frac{4}{12}$ we divide both the numerator and the denominator by 4:

$$\overset{\div 4}{\underset{\div 4}{\frac{4}{12} = \frac{1}{3}}}$$

$\frac{4}{12}$ and $\frac{1}{3}$ are equivalent fractions.

Warm up

1 Simplify these fractions using the method shown above.

a) $\frac{2}{4}$ b) $\frac{3}{9}$ c) $\frac{3}{12}$

2 Find the fractions in each of the circles that would simplify to the one written next to it. The first one has been done for you.

a) $\frac{1}{2}$ ⟶ $\left(\frac{1}{3} \quad \mathbf{\frac{2}{4}} \quad \frac{2}{6} \right)$

b) $\frac{1}{4}$ $\left(\frac{2}{6} \quad \frac{3}{9} \quad \frac{4}{10} \quad \frac{2}{8} \quad \frac{3}{4} \right)$

c) $\frac{1}{2}$ $\left(\frac{2}{6} \quad \frac{3}{6} \quad \frac{4}{10} \quad \frac{2}{8} \quad \frac{3}{8} \right)$

d) $\frac{1}{3}$ $\left(\frac{4}{3} \quad \frac{4}{12} \quad \frac{4}{6} \quad \frac{3}{4} \quad \frac{5}{8} \right)$

3 Simplify these fractions using the method shown on page 6.

a) $\frac{6}{8}$

b) $\frac{8}{10}$

c) $\frac{8}{12}$

4 Find the fractions in each of the circles that are the simplest forms of the fraction shown next to it. The first one has been done for you.

a) $\frac{5}{10}$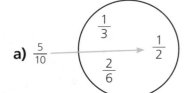

b) $\frac{2}{12}$

$\frac{1}{6}$ $\frac{3}{9}$

$\frac{4}{10}$ $\frac{2}{8}$

$\frac{3}{4}$

c) $\frac{3}{12}$

$\frac{1}{4}$ $\frac{1}{6}$

$\frac{1}{5}$ $\frac{2}{8}$

$\frac{3}{8}$

d) $\frac{6}{18}$

$\frac{1}{3}$ $\frac{4}{12}$

$\frac{1}{6}$ $\frac{5}{8}$

$\frac{3}{4}$

5 Simplify these fractions using the method shown on page 6.

a) $\frac{6}{21}$

b) $\frac{10}{15}$

c) $\frac{10}{25}$

6 Which fraction from the list below is equivalent to $\frac{3}{5}$?

$\frac{2}{3}$ $\frac{4}{5}$ $\frac{6}{10}$ $\frac{5}{3}$ $\frac{9}{12}$

7 The children in Year 4 sat a science test. In Class A, 5 out of 15 children passed the test and in Class B, 9 out of 18 children passed. Which class had the better results?

How did you do?

Simple fractions of amounts

To find a fraction of a number or amount we divide the amount by the denominator.

So, for example:

- to find $\frac{1}{2}$ of an amount, we divide by 2.
- to find $\frac{1}{3}$ of an amount, we divide by 3.
- to find $\frac{1}{4}$ of an amount, we divide by 4.

Example: Jamie has 24 football cards.
He gives his brother $\frac{1}{4}$ of them.
How many cards does Jamie give away?

$24 \div 4 = 6$

$\frac{1}{4}$ of $24 = 6$

Jamie gives away 6 cards.

Warm up

1. Find $\frac{1}{4}$ of these amounts.
   a) 12
   b) 28
   c) 16

2. Find $\frac{1}{3}$ of these amounts.
   a) 21
   b) 24
   c) 18

3. Find $\frac{1}{2}$ of these amounts.
   a) 12
   b) 24
   c) 16

4. Find $\frac{1}{5}$ of these amounts.
   a) 15
   b) 30
   c) 25

5. Hibba has 18 cookies. She gives her friend $\frac{1}{6}$ of them. How many cookies does Hibba give away?

6. Liam has 27 marbles. He gives his friend $\frac{1}{3}$ of them. How many marbles does Liam give away?

7. Draw this shape. Check carefully that you have the correct number of squares.

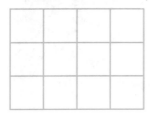

a) Shade $\frac{1}{6}$ blue

b) Shade $\frac{1}{4}$ green

c) Shade $\frac{1}{2}$ red

d) What fraction is not shaded?

Challenge yourself

8. Find

a) $\frac{1}{3}$ of 36   b) $\frac{1}{4}$ of 52   c) $\frac{1}{5}$ of 75

9. Farmer Doug has 24 sheep:

$\frac{1}{4}$ of them are white.

$\frac{1}{8}$ of them are black.

$\frac{1}{3}$ of them are brown.

$\frac{1}{6}$ of them have horns.

The rest are spotted.

a) How many of each type of sheep are there?

b) What fraction is spotted?

How did you do?

Harder fractions of amounts

Example: Hassan has 20 pencils. He lends $\frac{3}{4}$ to his friends. How many pencils does Hassan lend?

To find $\frac{3}{4}$ we need to find $\frac{1}{4}$ first.

$\frac{1}{4}$ of 20 = 20 ÷ 4 = 5

$\frac{1}{4}$ = of 20 = 5

We know that $\frac{3}{4} = \frac{1}{4} + \frac{1}{4} + \frac{1}{4}$

So $\frac{3}{4}$ of 20 = 5 + 5 + 5

$\frac{3}{4}$ = of 20 = 15

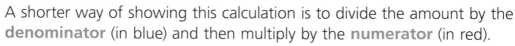

A shorter way of showing this calculation is to divide the amount by the **denominator** (in blue) and then multiply by the **numerator** (in red).

$\frac{3}{4}$ of 20

20 ÷ 4 = 5

5 × 3 = 15

$\frac{3}{4}$ of 20 = 15

Warm up

1 Find $\frac{3}{4}$ of these amounts.

a) 12

b) 16

c) 24

2 Find $\frac{2}{3}$ of these amounts.

a) 9

b) 18

c) 12

3 Find $\frac{3}{5}$ of these amounts.

a) 25

b) 15

c) 45

4 June threads 5 red beads and 4 yellow beads on to a string.

   a) What fraction of the beads is red?

   b) What fraction of the beads is yellow?

5 Meena has 36 coloured pencils. $\frac{4}{9}$ of the pencils are blue and $\frac{2}{6}$ are red. How many pencils are red and blue?

6 Peter has a number card.

He says '$\frac{5}{6}$ of my number is 30'.

48

Is Peter correct?

7 The teacher has a bag of 24 jelly beans. $\frac{5}{12}$ are strawberry flavoured, $\frac{3}{8}$ are banana flavoured and the rest are orange flavoured. How many jelly beans are orange flavoured?

8 Louisa has collected 24 buttons. She gives Petra $\frac{3}{8}$ of the buttons and Zara $\frac{2}{6}$ of the buttons. Who has the most buttons: Louisa, Petra or Zara?

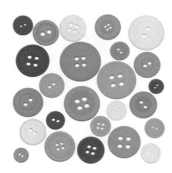

9 The greengrocer has a tray of 56 pieces of fruit. There are 21 bananas on the tray. What fraction of the fruit is made up of bananas?

How did you do?

Addition of fractions

We can add fractions with the same denominators:

$\frac{1}{5} + \frac{3}{5} = \frac{4}{5}$

$1\frac{1}{6} + \frac{4}{6} = 1\frac{5}{6}$

Example: Joanna has $1\frac{1}{4}$ pizzas and Rupa has $\frac{3}{4}$ of a pizza.
How much pizza do they have altogether?

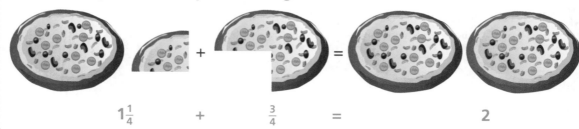

$1\frac{1}{4}$ + $\frac{3}{4}$ =   2

Warm up

1 Write the answers to these addition calculations. The first one has been done for you.

a) ▨ + ▨ $= \frac{1}{3} + \frac{1}{3} = \frac{2}{3}$

b) ▨ + ▨ =

c) ▨ + ▨ =

d) ▨ + ▨ =

2 Copy and complete these addition problems.

a) $\frac{3}{8} + \frac{2}{8} =$

b) $\frac{4}{12} + \frac{3}{12} =$

c) $\frac{9}{15} + \frac{2}{15} =$

3 Copy and complete these addition problems.

   a) $1\frac{3}{8} + \frac{4}{8} =$

   b) $2\frac{1}{5} + \frac{3}{5} =$

   c) $1\frac{2}{6} + \frac{3}{6} =$

4 Peter and Zara are chopping apples. Peter has $3\frac{3}{5}$ apples and Zara has $2\frac{1}{5}$ apples. How many apples do the children have altogether?

Challenge yourself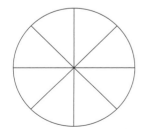

5 Copy and complete these number sentences. Replace the question marks with the correct numbers.

   a) $1\frac{2}{5} + \frac{?}{5} = 1\frac{4}{?}$

   b) $\frac{?}{6} + 1\frac{4}{6} = 1\frac{5}{?}$

   c) $1\frac{4}{8} + 1\frac{?}{8} = 2\frac{7}{?}$

6 Fabrice has $\frac{6}{8}$ of a pizza. Max has $\frac{5}{8}$ of another pizza. How much pizza do the boys have altogether? Copy and shade the shape below to help you to work it out.

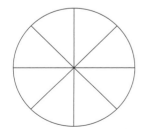
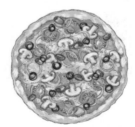

How did you do?

Subtraction of fractions

We can subtract fractions that have the same denominators.

$\frac{7}{8} - \frac{4}{8} = \frac{3}{8}$

$1\frac{3}{5} - \frac{2}{5} = 1\frac{1}{5}$

Example: Ranjit has a whole pizza and his dog eats $\frac{1}{4}$ of it.
How much pizza is left?

$\frac{4}{4}$ − $\frac{1}{4}$ = $\frac{3}{4}$

Warm up

1   Write the answers to these subtraction calculations. The first one has been done for you.

a) ▢▢▢ − ▢▢▢ $= \frac{2}{3} - \frac{1}{3} = \frac{1}{3}$

b) =

c) =

d) =

e) =

f) =

2 Copy and complete these subtraction problems.

a) $\frac{12}{14} - \frac{9}{14} =$

b) $\frac{7}{8} - \frac{2}{8} =$

c) $\frac{11}{16} - \frac{8}{16} =$

3 Copy and complete these subtraction problems.

a) $2\frac{7}{8} - \frac{4}{8} =$

b) $1\frac{6}{9} - 1\frac{2}{9} =$

c) $2\frac{4}{10} - \frac{1}{10} =$

4 Auntie Betty has baked an apple pie. She eats $\frac{1}{6}$ herself, gives $\frac{1}{6}$ to Uncle Bob and $\frac{3}{6}$ to Jimmy. How much pie is left for later?

5 Copy and complete these number sentences. Replace the question marks with the correct numbers.

a) $1\frac{3}{4} - \frac{2}{?} = 1\frac{?}{4}$

b) $1\frac{5}{7} - \frac{3}{?} = 1\frac{?}{7}$

c) $1\frac{9}{12} - 1\frac{5}{?} = \frac{?}{12}$

6 Great Aunty Minnie has baked a cake to share. She gives $\frac{3}{5}$ of the cake to her nephew and $\frac{1}{5}$ of the cake to her neighbour. Does she have any cake left for herself?

How did you do?

1 Copy these fraction pairs. Put either **<, >** or **=** between the fractions to make the statement correct.

  a) $\frac{3}{5}$ ☐ $\frac{7}{15}$

  b) $\frac{8}{12}$ ☐ $\frac{2}{3}$

  c) $\frac{4}{10}$ ☐ $\frac{3}{5}$

2 Simplify these fractions to their lowest form.

  a) $\frac{8}{20}$

  b) $\frac{12}{21}$

  c) $\frac{10}{15}$

3 Find $\frac{1}{3}$ of these amounts.

  a) 18

  b) 33

  c) 69

4 Find $\frac{2}{5}$ of these amounts.

  a) 30

  b) 45

  c) 70

5 Add these fractions.

  a) $\frac{7}{12} + \frac{3}{12} =$

  b) $\frac{3}{9} + \frac{4}{9} =$

  c) $\frac{14}{20} + \frac{5}{20} =$

6 Subtract these fractions.

  a) $\frac{9}{10} - \frac{5}{10} =$

  b) $\frac{12}{15} - \frac{9}{15} =$

  c) $\frac{8}{12} - \frac{7}{12} =$

7 Put these fractions in order from smallest to largest.

  $\frac{4}{5}$ $\frac{1}{10}$ $\frac{3}{5}$ $\frac{2}{10}$ $\frac{2}{5}$

8 Match the equivalent fractions. One has been done for you.

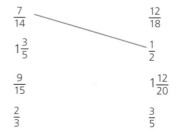

$\frac{7}{14}$ $\frac{12}{18}$

$1\frac{3}{5}$ $\frac{1}{2}$

$\frac{9}{15}$ $1\frac{12}{20}$

$\frac{2}{3}$ $\frac{3}{5}$

9 Tom has a bag of red and blue counters. $\frac{1}{4}$ of the counters are blue and he has 12 red counters.

  a) How many blue counters are there?

  b) How many counters are in the bag altogether?

10 Copy and complete these number sentences in your book.

  a) $1\frac{4}{9} + \dfrac{\boxed{?}}{9} = 1\frac{7}{9}$

  b) $1\dfrac{\boxed{?}}{12} - 1\frac{5}{12} = \frac{3}{12}$

  c) $1\frac{2}{11} + 1\dfrac{\boxed{?}}{11} = 2\frac{8}{11}$

  d) $1\frac{8}{9} - 1\dfrac{\boxed{?}}{9} = 1\frac{4}{9}$

Score ⬤ /10

1 Find the fraction inside the circle that is equivalent to the one written below the circle.

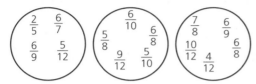

a) $\frac{2}{3}$ **b)** $\frac{3}{5}$ **c)** $\frac{5}{6}$

2 Simply these fractions to their most simple form.

a) $\frac{12}{18}$ **b)** $\frac{20}{25}$ **c)** $\frac{12}{20}$

3 Find $\frac{2}{3}$ of these amounts.

a) 24 **b)** 33 **c)** 48

4 What fraction of each shape is shaded? Simplify your answers where you can.

a) 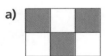 **b)**

c) **d)**

5 Copy and complete these calculations.

a) $\frac{4}{7} + \frac{2}{7} =$

b) $\frac{9}{12} - \frac{4}{12} =$

c) $\frac{9}{20} + \frac{5}{20} =$

d) $\frac{16}{19} - \frac{7}{19} =$

6 Match the equivalent fractions. One has been done for you.

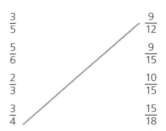

7 Copy these circles. Count them carefully. Draw a ring around $\frac{2}{3}$ of them.

8 Simplify these fractions to their most simple form.

a) $\frac{18}{30}$ **b)** $\frac{15}{18}$ **c)** $\frac{16}{20}$

9 Copy and complete these number sentences.

a) $1\frac{7}{15} + \frac{4}{15} =$

b) $\frac{21}{26} - \frac{18}{26} =$

c) $\frac{17}{35} + \frac{7}{35} =$

d) $\frac{68}{78} - \frac{9}{78} =$

10 Copy this shape then shade $\frac{2}{5}$ of it.

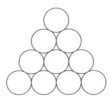

Score ⬤ / 10

Hundredths

We know that we can divide 1 whole into 10 equal parts. These are called **tenths** and one tenth is written as $\frac{1}{10}$ or 0.1.

We can also divide each $\frac{1}{10}$ into 10 equal parts. These are called **hundredths** and one hundredth is written as $\frac{1}{100}$ or 0.01.

Each whole has 10 tenths or 100 hundredths.

0	0.1	0.2	0.3	0.4	0.5	0.6	0.7	0.8	0.9	1
$\frac{1}{10}$	$\frac{1}{10}$	$\frac{1}{10}$	$\frac{1}{10}$	$\frac{1}{10}$	$\frac{1}{10}$	$\frac{1}{10}$	$\frac{1}{10}$	$\frac{1}{10}$	$\frac{1}{10}$	

0.9   1

$\frac{1}{10}$

$\frac{1}{100}$	$\frac{1}{100}$	$\frac{1}{100}$	$\frac{1}{100}$	$\frac{1}{100}$	$\frac{1}{100}$	$\frac{1}{100}$	$\frac{1}{100}$	$\frac{1}{100}$	$\frac{1}{100}$

0.91 0.92 0.93 0.94 0.95 0.96 0.97 0.98 0.99

Warm up

1 What are the next three fractions in each of the sequences?

a) $\frac{3}{100}$ $\frac{4}{100}$ $\frac{5}{100}$ ____ ____ ____

b) $\frac{25}{100}$ $\frac{26}{100}$ $\frac{27}{100}$ ____ ____ ____

c) $\frac{75}{100}$ $\frac{74}{100}$ $\frac{73}{100}$ ____ ____ ____

2 Fill in the gaps in the sequences.

a) $\frac{36}{100}$ ____ $\frac{38}{100}$ ____ ____

b) $\frac{51}{100}$ ____ ____ $\frac{48}{100}$ ____

c) $\frac{89}{100}$ ____ ____ ____ ____

3 What numbers are at **a**, **b**, **c** and **d** on the number line?

4 What numbers are at **a**, **b**, **c** and **d** on the number line?

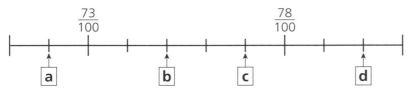

Challenge yourself

5 Put these numbers in order from smallest to largest.

$1\frac{23}{100}$ $\frac{35}{100}$ $1\frac{45}{100}$ $\frac{75}{100}$ $1\frac{5}{100}$

6 What numbers are at **a**, **b**, **c** and **d** on the number line?

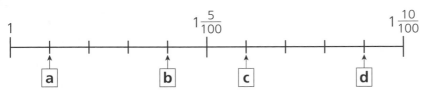

7 Order these fractions from smallest to largest.

$\frac{7}{10}$ $\frac{3}{100}$ $\frac{5}{10}$ $\frac{75}{100}$ $\frac{2}{10}$

How did you do?

Hundredths as decimals

We know the value a digit has by looking at its position.

Example: The number 1.32 has 1 unit, 3 tenths and 2 hundredths.

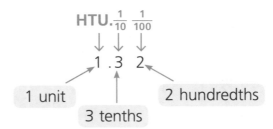

[tip – think of numbers with hundredths as money; for example, 1.32 = £ 1.32]

Warm up

1 What value does the digit 5 have in these numbers?

Example: 54.6 has 5 tens.

a) 15.29

b) 34.50

c) 76.15

d) 12.58

2 Write these numbers in figures.

a) seven point four two.

b) six point zero seven.

c) four point three.

3 Write these numbers in words.

a) 3.51

b) 2.08

c) 9.4

4 What numbers are at **a**, **b**, **c** and **d** on the number line?

1.10   1.15   1.20

5 Match these fractions to their decimal equivalents.

1.75   0.3

$\frac{7}{100}$ $1\frac{75}{100}$

0.8   0.07

$\frac{3}{10}$ $\frac{80}{100}$

Challenge yourself

6 Put these numbers in order from smallest to largest.

1.25   0.35   1.45   0.75   1.05

7 What numbers are at **a**, **b**, **c** and **d** on the number line?

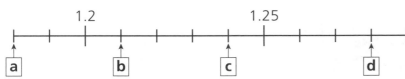

1.2   1.25

8 What numbers are at **a**, **b**, **c** and **d** on the number line?

0.04   0.09

How did you do?

Decimal equivalents

We can find decimal equivalents for fractions.

Example: We know that $\frac{1}{10}$ means '1 whole divided into 10 equal pieces'.

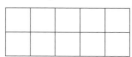

When we divide 1 by 10 we get 0.1

$1 \div 10 = 0.1$

0.1 is the decimal equivalent of $\frac{1}{10}$

When we divide 1 by 100 we get 0.01

$1 \div 100 = 0.01$

0.01 is the decimal equivalent of $\frac{1}{100}$

0.1 and 0.01 are called **decimals** or **decimal fractions** because they have a decimal point.

1.5 is the decimal equivalent of $1\frac{1}{2}$

Warm up

1. Write the decimal equivalents for these fractions.

   a) $\frac{3}{10}$

   b) $\frac{7}{10}$

   c) $\frac{4}{10}$

2. Write the decimal equivalents for these fractions.

   a) $\frac{9}{100}$

   b) $\frac{2}{100}$

   c) $\frac{5}{100}$

3. Convert these decimals to fractions.

   a) 0.05

   b) 0.97

   c) 1.35

Answers

a) $\frac{1}{3}$ b) $\frac{2}{4}$ or $\frac{1}{2}$ c) $\frac{2}{6}$ or $\frac{1}{3}$

d) $\frac{4}{8}$ or $\frac{1}{2}$ e) $\frac{3}{6}$ or $\frac{1}{2}$

a) $\frac{2}{4}, \frac{3}{6}, \frac{4}{8}, \frac{5}{10}, \frac{6}{12}$ b) $\frac{2}{8}, \frac{3}{12}$ c) $\frac{6}{8}, \frac{9}{12}$ d) $\frac{2}{10}$

a) $\frac{1}{5}$ b) $\frac{2}{10}$ c) $\frac{4}{12}$

$\frac{1}{6}$ $\frac{1}{5}$ $\frac{1}{4}$ $\frac{3}{8}$ $\frac{1}{2}$ $\frac{3}{4}$

a) $\frac{2}{3} < \frac{9}{12}$ b) $\frac{3}{8} < \frac{2}{4}$ c) $\frac{5}{10} > \frac{2}{5}$

$\frac{12}{24}$

a) $\frac{1}{2}$ b) $\frac{1}{3}$ c) $\frac{1}{4}$

a) $\frac{2}{4}$ b) $\frac{2}{8}$

c) $\frac{3}{6}$ d) $\frac{4}{12}$

a) $\frac{3}{4}$ b) $\frac{4}{5}$ c) $\frac{2}{3}$

a) $\frac{1}{2}$ b) $\frac{1}{6}$

c) $\frac{1}{4}$ d) $\frac{1}{3}$

a) $\frac{2}{7}$ b) $\frac{2}{3}$ c) $\frac{2}{5}$

$\frac{6}{10}$

Class B; $\frac{1}{2}$ passed (Class A only $\frac{1}{3}$ passed).

a) 3   b) 7   c) 4

a) 7   b) 8   c) 6

a) 6   b) 12   c) 8

a) 3   b) 6   c) 5

3

9

a) 2 squares shaded blue

b) 3 squares shaded green

c) 6 squares shaded red

d) $\frac{1}{12}$

a) 12   b) 13   c) 15

a) 6 white, 3 black, 8 brown, 4 horns, 3 spotted

b) $\frac{1}{8}$

a) 9   b) 12   c) 18

a) 6   b) 12   c) 8

a) 15   b) 9   c) 27

a) $\frac{5}{9}$ b) $\frac{4}{9}$

16 red and 12 blue

No, $\frac{5}{6}$ of 48 is 40.

5

Petra (she has 9 buttons)

$\frac{3}{8}$

1. a) $\frac{2}{3}$ b) $\frac{3}{4}$

   c) $\frac{5}{8}$ d) $\frac{3}{6}$ $\left(\frac{1}{2}\right)$

2. a) $\frac{5}{8}$ b) $\frac{7}{12}$ c) $\frac{11}{15}$

3. a) $1\frac{7}{8}$ b) $2\frac{4}{5}$ c) $1\frac{5}{6}$

4. $5\frac{4}{5}$

5. a) $1\frac{2}{5} + \frac{2}{5} = 1\frac{4}{5}$

   b) $\frac{1}{6} + 1\frac{4}{6} = 1\frac{5}{6}$

   c) $1\frac{4}{8} + 1\frac{3}{8} = 2\frac{7}{8}$

6. $\frac{11}{8}$ or $1\frac{3}{8}$

1. a) $\frac{1}{3}$ b) $\frac{1}{6}$ c) $\frac{1}{4}$

   d) $\frac{3}{8}$ e) $\frac{3}{12}$ f) $\frac{3}{5}$

2. a) $\frac{3}{14}$ b) $\frac{5}{8}$ c) $\frac{3}{16}$

3. a) $2\frac{3}{8}$ b) $\frac{4}{9}$ c) $2\frac{3}{10}$

4. $\frac{1}{6}$

5. a) $1\frac{3}{4} - \frac{2}{4} = 1\frac{1}{4}$

   b) $1\frac{5}{7} - \frac{3}{7} = 1\frac{2}{7}$

   c) $1\frac{9}{12} - 1\frac{5}{12} = \frac{4}{12}$

6. yes, $\frac{1}{5}$

1. a) $\frac{3}{5} > \frac{7}{15}$ b) $\frac{8}{12} = \frac{2}{3}$ c) $\frac{4}{10} < \frac{3}{5}$

2. a) $\frac{2}{5}$ b) $\frac{4}{7}$ c) $\frac{2}{3}$

3. a) 6   b) 11   c) 23

4. a) 12   b) 18   c) 28

5. a) $\frac{10}{12}$ or $\frac{5}{6}$ b) $\frac{7}{9}$ c) $\frac{19}{20}$

6. a) $\frac{4}{10}$ or $\frac{2}{5}$ b) $\frac{3}{15}$ or $\frac{1}{5}$ c) $\frac{1}{12}$

7. $\frac{1}{10}$ $\frac{2}{10}$ $\frac{2}{5}$ $\frac{3}{5}$ $\frac{4}{5}$

8.

$\frac{7}{14}$		$\frac{12}{18}$
$1\frac{3}{5}$		$\frac{1}{2}$
$\frac{9}{15}$		$1\frac{12}{20}$
$\frac{2}{3}$		$\frac{3}{5}$

9. a) 4   b) 16

10. a) $1\frac{4}{9} + \frac{3}{9} = 1\frac{7}{9}$

    b) $1\frac{8}{12} - 1\frac{5}{12} = \frac{3}{12}$

    c) $1\frac{2}{11} + 1\frac{6}{11} = 2\frac{8}{11}$

    d) $1\frac{8}{9} - \frac{4}{9} = 1\frac{4}{9}$

Page 17

1. **a)** $\frac{6}{9}$ **b)** $\frac{6}{10}$ **c)** $\frac{10}{12}$

2. **a)** $\frac{2}{3}$ **b)** $\frac{4}{5}$ **c)** $\frac{3}{5}$

3. **a)** 16   **b)** 22   **c)** 32

4. **a)** $\frac{3}{6} = \frac{1}{2}$ **b)** $\frac{4}{10} = \frac{2}{5}$

     c) $\frac{3}{8}$ **d)** $\frac{3}{5}$

5. **a)** $\frac{6}{7}$ **b)** $\frac{5}{12}$

     c) $\frac{14}{20} = \frac{7}{10}$ **d)** $\frac{9}{19}$

6. $\frac{3}{5}$ $\frac{9}{12}$ $\frac{5}{6}$ $\frac{9}{15}$ $\frac{2}{3}$ $\frac{10}{15}$ $\frac{3}{4}$ $\frac{15}{18}$ *(matched with connecting lines)*

7. 8 circles ringed

8. **a)** $\frac{3}{5}$ **b)** $\frac{5}{6}$ **c)** $\frac{4}{5}$

9. **a)** $1\frac{11}{15}$ **b)** $\frac{3}{26}$

     c) $\frac{24}{35}$ **d)** $\frac{59}{78}$

10. 4 circles shaded

Pages 18–19

1. **a)** $\frac{6}{100}, \frac{7}{100}, \frac{8}{100}$

     b) $\frac{28}{100}, \frac{29}{100}, \frac{30}{100}$

     c) $\frac{72}{100}, \frac{71}{100}, \frac{70}{100}$

2. **a)** $\frac{36}{100}, \mathbf{\frac{37}{100}}, \frac{38}{100}, \mathbf{\frac{39}{100}}, \mathbf{\frac{40}{100}}$

     b) $\frac{51}{100}, \mathbf{\frac{50}{100}}, \mathbf{\frac{49}{100}}, \frac{48}{100}, \mathbf{\frac{47}{100}}$

     c) $\frac{89}{100}, \mathbf{\frac{90}{100}}, \mathbf{\frac{91}{100}}, \mathbf{\frac{92}{100}}, \frac{93}{100}$

3. **a)** $\frac{29}{100}$ **b)** $\frac{32}{100}$

     c) $\frac{36}{100}$ **d)** $\frac{38}{100}$

4. **a)** $\frac{72}{100}$ **b)** $\frac{75}{100}$

     c) $\frac{77}{100}$ **d)** $\frac{80}{100}$

5. $\frac{35}{100}, \frac{75}{100}, 1\frac{5}{100}, 1\frac{23}{100}, 1\frac{45}{100}$

6. **a)** $1\frac{1}{100}$ **b)** $1\frac{4}{100}$

     c) $1\frac{6}{100}$ **d)** $1\frac{9}{100}$

7. **a)** $\frac{3}{100}, \frac{2}{10}, \frac{5}{10}, \frac{7}{10}, \frac{75}{100}$

Pages 20–21

1. **a)** 5 units   **b)** 5 tenths
     c) 5 hundredths   **d)** 5 tenths

2. **a)** 7.42   **b)** 6.07   **c)** 4.3

3. **a)** three point five one
     b) two point zero eight
     c) nine point four

4. **a)** 1.12   **b)** 1.14
     c) 1.17   **d)** 1.19

5. 1.75   0.3 $\frac{7}{100}$ $1\frac{75}{100}$ 0.8   0.07 $\frac{3}{10}$ $\frac{80}{100}$ *(matched with connecting lines)*

6. 0.35   0.75   1.05   1.25   1.45

7. **a)** 1.18   **b)** 1.21
     c) 1.24   **d)** 1.28

8. **a)** 0.02   **b)** 0.05
     c) 0.08   **d)** 0.12

Pages 22–23

1. **a)** 0.3   **b)** 0.7   **c)** 0.4

2. **a)** 0.09   **b)** 0.02   **c)** 0.05

3 **a)** $\frac{5}{100}$ **b)** $\frac{97}{100}$ **c)** $1\frac{35}{100}$

4 **a)** 0.23   **b)** 0.54   **c)** 0.98

5. **a)** 0.1   **b)** 0.3
     c) 0.6   **d)** 0.9

6. 0.01 $\frac{3}{4}$ $\frac{5}{10}$ 0.25   0.75   0.05 $\frac{1}{4}$ $\frac{1}{100}$ $\frac{5}{100}$ 0.5 *(matched with connecting lines)*

7. $\frac{2}{10}$ 0.3 $\frac{4}{10}$ $\frac{5}{10}$ 0.9

8. 0.05   0.06 $\frac{7}{100}$ $\frac{8}{100}$ $\frac{9}{100}$

9. **a)** 0.53   **b)** 0.56
     c) 0.59   **d)** 0.63

Pages 24–25

1. **a)** 0.7   **b)** 0.4   **c)** 0.2

2. **a)** 0.05   **b)** 0.03   **c)** 0.08

3. **a)** 0.7   **b)** 10   **c)** 36

4. **a)** 2.3   **b)** 4.5   **c)** 1.6

5. 0.7 km

6. 0.3 m

7. 0.6 m

8. **a)** 6.7   **b)** 4.5   **c)** 2.9

9. **a)** 0.05 m   **b)** 0.08 m   **c)** 0.02 m

10. **a)** 0.03   **b)** 10   **c)** 4.5

Pages 26–27

1. **a)** 0.08   **b)** 0.03   **c)** 0.05

2. **a)** 0.46   **b)** 0.38   **c)** 0.51

3. **a)** 0.24   **b)** 0.07   **c)** 0.99

4. **a)** $32 \div \mathbf{100} = 0.32$
     b) $\mathbf{2} \div 100 = 0.02$
     c) $56 \div 100 = \mathbf{0.56}$

5. 0.08 m

6. 0.26 miles

7. 0.65 litres

8. 0.3 m and 0.03 m

9. 0.78 cm

10. 0.25 m

Page 28

1. a) $\frac{37}{100}, \frac{38}{100}, \frac{39}{100}$

   b) $\frac{70}{100}, \frac{69}{100}, \frac{68}{100}$

2. 2.5 litres
3. a) 0.05   b) 0.23   c) 0.14   d) 0.99
4. a) $32 \div 100 = \mathbf{0.32}$
   b) $65 \div \mathbf{100} = 0.65$
   c) $\mathbf{3} \div 100 = 0.03$
5. a) 0.5   b) 0.03   c) 0.9   d) 0.45
6. a) 26.10   b) 26.13   c) 26.16   d) 26.17
7. 0.27 m
8. a) $45 \div 10 = \mathbf{4.5}$
   b) $23 \div \mathbf{10} = 2.3$
   c) $\mathbf{69} \div 10 = 6.9$
9. 0.06
10. a) $\frac{5}{10} = \frac{1}{2}$ b) $\frac{75}{100} = \frac{3}{4}$ c) $\frac{25}{100} = \frac{1}{4}$

Page 29

1. a) $\frac{40}{100}$ b) $\frac{70}{100}$

   c) $1\frac{30}{100}$ d) $1\frac{60}{100}$

2. a) 10   b) 6   c) 9.9
3. a) 0.66   b) 0.69   c) 0.72   d) 0.77
4. a) 0.8   b) 0.2   c) 0.5
5. a) $\frac{5}{100}\left(\frac{1}{20}\right)$ b) $\frac{65}{100}\left(\frac{13}{20}\right)$ c) $\frac{4}{10}\left(\frac{2}{5}\right)$
6. a) $\mathbf{34} \div 10 = 3.4$
   b) $7 \div 100 = \mathbf{0.07}$
   c) $56 \div \mathbf{100} = 0.56$
7. a) 0.31   b) 0.34
   c) 0.37   d) 0.42
8. a) $\frac{31}{100}$ b) $\frac{34}{100}$
   c) $\frac{37}{100}$ d) $\frac{42}{100}$
9. a) $\frac{30}{100}, \frac{31}{100}, \frac{32}{100}$
   b) 0.05, 0.04, 0.03
   c) 0.90, 0.89, 0.88
10. a) $\frac{85}{100}$ or $\frac{17}{20}$

    b) $\frac{8}{10}$ or $\frac{80}{100}$

    c) $\frac{8}{100}$ or $\frac{4}{50}$ or $\frac{2}{25}$

Pages 30–31

1. a) 1   b) 2   c) 2
2. a) 4   b) 3   c) 4
3. Decimal   Rounds to

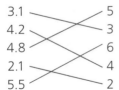

4. a) 36   b) 136   c) 70
   d) 170   e) 22   f) 27
5.

Number	Rounded to the nearest whole number
14.3	**14**
27.6	28
13.2	13
127.7	128
58.5	59

6. Any number from 5.5 to 6.4 inclusive.

Pages 32–33

1. a) 4.75   b) 1.27   c) 7.67
2. 0.31   0.33   0.34   0.36   0.38
3. £1.55, £1.56, £1.65, £3.55, £3.56
4. a) 3 tenths   b) 3 hundredths   c) 3 tens
5. a) 3.01   b) 1.56   c) 9.98
6. a) 3.07   b) 3.09
   c) 3.12   d) 3.13
7. 0.12   0.29   0.37   0.45   0.63   0.78
8. 1.33   1.53   3.13   3.15   3.35   33.51
9. Javid
10. a) $67.43 > 67.4\mathbf{2}$
    b) $32.\mathbf{1}5 < 32.25$
    c) $45.\mathbf{3}7 > 45.27$
11. a) false   b) true   c) true

Pages 34–35

1. a) $\frac{1}{2}$ b) $\frac{3}{4}$ c) $\frac{1}{4}$
2. a) 0.75   b) 0.25   c) 0.5
3.

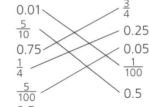

4. 0.5
5. 0.75 m
6. 0.25
7. $\frac{5}{100} = 0.05, \frac{1}{10} = 0.1, \frac{1}{4} = 0.25, \frac{5}{10} = 0.5, \frac{3}{4} = 0.75$

Pages 36–37

1. **B** and **D** have $\frac{1}{3}$ shaded
2. Any 4 squares shaded
3. a) $\frac{1}{3} = \frac{4}{12}$ b) $\frac{1}{4} = \frac{2}{8}$ c) $\frac{2}{5} = \frac{4}{10}$
4. 10 balls
5. $\frac{6}{9} = \frac{2}{3}$
6. $\frac{1}{3}, \frac{2}{5}, \frac{3}{8}, \frac{5}{12}$ or equivalents

7. $\frac{1}{3}$ of 150 is 50

$\frac{1}{2}$ of 90 is 45

$\frac{1}{5}$ of 150 is 30

$\frac{1}{4}$ of 160 is 40

8. **a)** $\frac{8}{9}$ **b)** $\frac{3}{12} = \frac{1}{4}$

c) $\frac{13}{16}$ **d)** $\frac{6}{15} = \frac{2}{5}$

9. 75

10. $\frac{6}{14} = \frac{3}{7} = \frac{15}{35}$

11. 24

12. **a)** $\frac{1}{5}$ **b)** $\frac{2}{5}$ **c)** $\frac{2}{5}$

13. £3.10 or £3 and 10p

14. 12

15. $\frac{3}{5}$

Pages 38–39

1. **a)** 0.56, 0.57, 0.58, **0.59**, **0.60**, **0.61**
b) 0.83, 0.82, 0.81, **0.8**, **0.79**, **0.78**
c) 0.18, 0.19, **0.2**, 0.21, **0.22**, **0.23**

2. **a)** 0.2 **b)** 3.6 **c)** 1.8

3. **a)** 76 **b)** 20 **c)** 38

4. **a)** 0.3 **b)** 0.6 **c)** 0.5
d) 0.2 **e)** 0.4

5. **a)** 0.07 **b)** 0.25 **c)** 0.2

6. **a)** 4.9 **b)** 5.5
c) 5.8 **d)** 6.1

7. **a)** 0.3 **b)** 0.09 **c)** 0.7
d) 0.26 **e)** 0.03

8. **a)** $\frac{3}{100}$ **b)** $\frac{2}{100}\left(\frac{1}{50}\right)$ **c)** $\frac{9}{10}$
d) $\frac{34}{100}\left(\frac{17}{50}\right)$ **e)** $\frac{75}{100}\left(\frac{3}{4}\right)$

9. 6 bricks shaded

10. $\frac{6}{10}$ 0.7
0.75   0.09
$\frac{7}{10}$ $\frac{3}{4}$
$\frac{9}{100}$ 0.06

11. **a)** 0.6 2.3 2.6 3.2 6.2
b) 14.26 14.60 41.61 14.62

12. **a)** 0.45 **b)** 0.16 **c)** 0.03

13. **a)** 2.99 **b)** 3.05
c) 3.08 **d)** 3.11

14. **a)** 4

15. 5 pieces of fudge

Page 40

1. **a)** 3.54 **b)** 0.30 **c)** 7.32

2. **a)** $1.00 = \frac{1}{1}$ **b)** $0.25 = \frac{1}{4}$
c) $0.5 = \frac{1}{2}$ **d)** $0.75 = \frac{3}{4}$

3. £0.04 £0.34 £0.43 £3.45 £4.53

4. **a)** 3 **b)** 77 **c)** 15

5. **a)** 32p **b)** 165p **c)** 5p

6. 0.10 0.25 $\frac{1}{2}$ $\frac{3}{4}$ 0.90

7. **a)** 0.45 m **b)** 0.5 m **c)** 0.93 m

8. Any number from 4.5 to 5.4 inclusive

9. 0.2 litres

10. **a)** 8 **b)** 32
c) 177 **d)** 100

Page 41

1. **a)** 6 **b)** 6 **c)** 3

2. **a)** 4.6 **b)** 7.3 **c)** 8.7

3. 3.4, 3.7, 3.9, 7.3, 7.5

4. £2.45, £2.54, £ 4.20, £4.25, £5.42

5. $\frac{1}{2} = 0.5$, $\frac{1}{4} = 0.25$, $\frac{3}{4} = 0.75$, $\frac{4}{4} = 1.0$

6. £1.50

7. 1.5 m

8. 0.75 m = 75 cm, 0.7 kg = 700 g, 0.75 km = 750 m

9. 0.3 m, 0.33 cm, 35 cm, 300 cm, 350 cm

10. 25p, 50p, £0.52, £1.25, 152p

Pages 42–43

1. $\frac{8}{12}$ and $\frac{2}{3}$

$\frac{9}{12}$ and $\frac{3}{4}$

$1\frac{2}{10}$ and $1\frac{1}{5}$

2. **a)** False **b)** True **c)** True

3. $\frac{2}{4}$ and $\frac{4}{8}$

4. 0.02, $\frac{7}{100}$, 0.25, $\frac{70}{100}$, $\frac{3}{4}$

5. 0.23 km

6. 0.96 litres

7. 64

8. $\frac{4}{5}$ and $\frac{2}{3}$

9. 0.3 m

10. **a)** $\frac{7}{15}$ red and $\frac{8}{15}$ blue
b) 17
c) $\frac{10}{17}$

11. $\frac{5}{12}$

12. 0.88 m

13. Millie 3.76 km

14. 4

15. £3.20

16. 8

17. 2.5 m

18. 0.25 km or 250 m

19. Freya 0.270 kg

20. 3.45 km, 3.54 km, 4.53 km, 5.34 km, 5.43 km

4 Convert these fractions to decimals.

a) $\frac{23}{100}$

b) $\frac{54}{100}$

c) $\frac{98}{100}$

5 What decimals are at **a**, **b**, **c** and **d** on the number line?

6 Copy and match the decimals and fractions. One has been done for you.

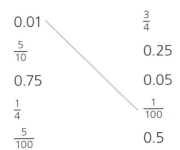

0.01	$\frac{3}{4}$
$\frac{5}{10}$	0.25
0.75	0.05
$\frac{1}{4}$	$\frac{1}{100}$
$\frac{5}{100}$	0.5

Challenge yourself

7 Order these decimals and fractions from smallest to biggest.

$\frac{5}{10}$ 0.3 $\frac{2}{10}$ 0.9 $\frac{4}{10}$

8 Order these decimals and fractions from smallest to biggest.

$\frac{9}{100}$ 0.06 $\frac{8}{100}$ 0.05 $\frac{7}{100}$

9 What decimals are at **a**, **b**, **c** and **d** on the number line?

How did you do?

Divide numbers by 10

If we divide units by 10 we get tenths.

To divide numbers by 10 we move the digits **one place** to the **right**.

Example: 3 ÷ 10

$$H \ T \ U \ . \ \tfrac{1}{10} \ \tfrac{1}{100}$$

Moves one place to the right ⟶
$$3 \downarrow$$
$$0 \ . \ 3$$

3 ÷ 10 = 0.3

0.3 has no units and 3 tenths

If we divide tenths by 10 we get hundredths.

Example: 0.3 ÷ 10

$$H \ T \ U \ . \ \tfrac{1}{10} \ \tfrac{1}{100}$$

Moves one place to the right ⟶
$$0 \ . \ 3 \downarrow$$
$$0 \ . \ 0 \ 3$$

We need to put a place holder after the decimal point

0.3 ÷ 100 = 0.03

0.03 has no units, no tenths and 3 hundredths

Example: Bert walks the same distance every week. After 10 weeks he has walked 24 km. How far did he walk each week?

$$H \ T \ U \ . \ \tfrac{1}{10} \ \tfrac{1}{100}$$
$$\downarrow \ \downarrow \qquad \quad \ \downarrow$$

Moves one place to the right ⟶
$$2 \ 4 \downarrow$$
$$2 \ . \ 4$$

Bert walked 2.4 km each week.

1. Divide these whole numbers by 10.

   a) 7   **b)** 4   **c)** 2

2. Divide these fractions by 10.

   a) 0.5   **b)** 0.3   **c)** 0.8

3. Copy and complete these number sequences.

   a) $7 \div 10 = \boxed{}$ **b)** $0.2 \div \boxed{} = 0.02$ **c)** $\boxed{} \div 10 = 3.6$

Test yourself

4. Divide these numbers by 10.

   a) 23   **b)** 45   **c)** 16

5. Brogan ran 7 km in a race. His little brother Jo ran the first $\frac{1}{10}$ of the race with him. How far did Jo run?

6. Jill has 3 metres of ribbon. She cuts it into 10 equal pieces. How long is each piece of ribbon?

7. The fisherman has 6 m of fishing line. He cuts it into 10 equal pieces. How long is each piece?

Challenge yourself

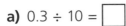

8. Find $\frac{1}{10}$ of these amounts.

   a) 67   **b)** 45   **c)** 29

9. Farmer Doug has three lengths of wire to mend his hen house. Piece **a** is 0.5 m long, piece **b** is 0.8 m and piece **c** is 0.2 m. His neighbour borrows $\frac{1}{10}$ of each piece. How long is each piece of his neighbour's wire?

10. Copy and complete these number sequences.

    a) $0.3 \div 10 = \boxed{}$

    b) $60 \div \boxed{} = 6$

    c) $\boxed{} \div 10 = 0.45$

Divide by 100

When we divide single-digit numbers by 100 we get **hundredths**.

$$H \; T \; U \; . \; \tfrac{1}{10} \; \tfrac{1}{100}$$

Moves two places to the right → 4

0 . 0 4

We need to put place holders before the number

Example: Leona has a roll of ribbon 36 metres long. She cuts it into 100 equal lengths. How long is each length?

To divide numbers by 100 we move the digits **two places** to the **right**.

$$H \; T \; U \; . \; \tfrac{1}{10} \; \tfrac{1}{100}$$

Moves two places to the right → 3 6

0 . 3 6

$36 \div 100 = 0.36$

Leona's ribbon pieces are 0.36 metres long.

Warm up

1. Divide these numbers by 100.

   a) 8

   b) 3

   c) 5

2. Divide these numbers by 100.

   a) 46

   b) 38

   c) 51

3 Divide these numbers by 100.

    a) 24

    b) 7

    c) 99

4 Copy and complete these number sentences.

    a) $32 \div \boxed{} = 0.32$

    b) $\boxed{} \div 100 = 0.02$

    c) $56 \div 100 = \boxed{}$

5 Peter cuts an 8-metre rope into 100 equal pieces. How long is each piece?

6 A marathon race is 26 miles long. How far have I run if I run $\frac{1}{100}$ of this distance? Give your answer in miles.

Challenge yourself

7 Sami's mum fills the bath with 65 litres of warm water. She adds $\frac{1}{100}$ of this amount of bubble bath. How much bubble bath does she add to the water?

8 Imogen has a 6-metre roll of ribbon. She cuts half of it into 10 equal pieces and the other half into 100 equal pieces. How long is each of the different pieces?

9 Rhys builds a tower of 100 bricks. The tower is 78 cm tall. How tall is one brick?

10 Junit lays 100 plates in a line along a table. The line of plates is 25 metres long. How wide is each plate in metres?

How did you do?

Progress test 3

1 What are the next three terms in these sequences?

a) $\frac{34}{100}$, $\frac{35}{100}$, $\frac{36}{100}$ _____, _____, _____

b) $\frac{73}{100}$, $\frac{72}{100}$, $\frac{71}{100}$ _____, _____, _____

2 Kevin's fish tank has 25 litres of water in it. Emily pours out $\frac{1}{10}$ of the water. How much does she pour out?

3 Find $\frac{1}{100}$ of these amounts.

a) 5

b) 23

c) 14

d) 99

4 Copy and complete these statements.

a) $32 \div 100 = \boxed{}$

b) $65 \div \boxed{} = 0.65$

c) $\boxed{} \div 100 = 0.03$

5 Write the decimal equivalents for these fractions.

a) $\frac{5}{10}$

b) $\frac{3}{100}$

c) $\frac{9}{10}$

d) $\frac{45}{100}$

6 What decimals are at **a**, **b**, **c** and **d** on the number line?

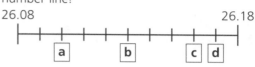

7 Emily has 27 m of rope. She cuts it into 100 equal pieces. How long is each piece?

8 Copy and complete these statements.

a) $45 \div 10 = \boxed{}$

b) $23 \div \boxed{} = 2.3$

c) $\boxed{} \div 10 = 6.9$

9 What is $\frac{1}{10}$ of 0.6?

10 Write the fractions that are equivalent to these decimals.

a) 0.5

b) 0.75

c) 0.25

Score ⬤ /10

Progress test 4

1 What fractions are at **a**, **b**, **c** and **d** on the number line?

2 Copy and complete these number sentences.

a) $48 \div \boxed{} = 4.8$

b) $\boxed{} \div 100 = 0.06$

c) $99 \div 10 = \boxed{}$

3 What decimals are at **a, b, c** and **d** on the number line?

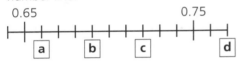

4 Write these fractions as decimals.

a) $\frac{8}{10}$

b) $\frac{2}{10}$

c) $\frac{5}{10}$

5 Write these decimals as fractions.

a) 0.05

b) 0.65

c) 0.4

6 Copy and complete these number sentences.

a) $\boxed{} \div 10 = 3.4$

b) $7 \div 100 = \boxed{}$

c) $56 \div \boxed{} = 0.56$

Look at this number line, then answer questions 7 and 8.

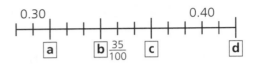

7 Write the decimals at **a**, **b**, **c** and **d** on the number line.

8 Write the fractions at **a**, **b**, **c** and **d** on the number line.

9 Copy and complete these sequences.

a) $\frac{27}{100}$ $\frac{28}{100}$ $\frac{29}{100}$ ____ ____ ____

b) 0.08   0.07   0.06 ____ ____ ____

c) 0.93   0.92   0.91 ____ ____ ____

10 Copy and complete these fractions.

a) $\dfrac{\boxed{}}{\boxed{}} = 0.85$

b) $\dfrac{\boxed{}}{\boxed{}} = 0.8$

c) $\dfrac{\boxed{}}{\boxed{}} = 0.08$

Score $\bigcirc$ /10

29

Rounding decimals

Sometimes we round numbers to make them easier to work with.

We can round whole numbers 'to the nearest...' either 10, 100, 1000, etc.

We can round decimals to the nearest whole number.

To round **2.7** to the nearest **whole number** we look at the tenths column (in red).

$$H\ T\ U\ .\ \frac{1}{10}$$
$$2\ .\ 7$$

If the tenths digit is less than 5, we round down.

If the tenths digit it 5 or more, we round up.

In 2.7 the tenths digit is a 7 so we round up.

From the number line we can see that 2.7 is nearer to 3 than 2.
We round 2.7 to 3.

Warm up

1 Using the number line to help you, round these decimals to the nearest whole number.

    a) 1.2

    b) 1.8

    c) 1.5

2 Round these numbers to the nearest whole number.

    a) 3.5

    b) 3.2

    c) 3.8

3 Match these numbers to their rounded partners. The first one has been done for you.

Decimal	Rounds to
3.1	5
4.2	3
4.8	6
2.1	4
5.5	2

4 Round these numbers to the nearest whole number.

a) 36.2   **b)** 136.2   **c)** 69.9   **d)** 169.9

e) 21.7   **f)** 27.1

Challenge yourself

5 Round these numbers to the nearest whole number. The first one has been done for you.

Number	Rounded to the nearest whole number
14.3	**14**
27.6	
13.2	
127.7	
58.5	

6 Mike thinks of a decimal less than 8. He rounds it to the nearest whole number and gets the answer 6. What could Mike's decimal number have been?

How did you do?

Compare decimals

When comparing decimals we need to look at each digit in turn.

Example: Which is greater: 3.45 or 3.47?

To find out, we need to look at each digit in turn.

$$H \; T \; U \; . \; \frac{1}{10} \; \frac{1}{100}$$

3 . 4 5

3 . 4 7

Both numbers have 3 units, so we need to look at the tenths.

Both numbers have 4 tenths, so we need to look at the hundredths.

3.45 has 5 hundredths and 3.47 has 7 hundredths.

3.47 is greater than 3.45

3.47 > 3.45

Warm up

1. Look at the number pairs below. Write the biggest number from each pair.

   a) 4.75 or 4.73

   b) 1.27 or 1.24

   c) 7.61 or 7.67

2. Put these numbers in order from smallest to largest.

   0.31   0.36   0.33   0.38   0.34

3. 5 children empty their money boxes. Put their savings in order from smallest to largest.

£ 3.56   £ 1.56   £ 1.65   £ 1.55   £ 3.55

4. What value does the digit 3 have in these numbers?

   a) 4.32

   b) 40.03

   c) 432.04

5 Look at the number pairs. Write the smaller number from each pair.

    a) 3.01   3.1

    b) 1.56   1.65

    c) 9.99   9.98

6 What numbers are at **a**, **b**, **c** and **d** on the number line?

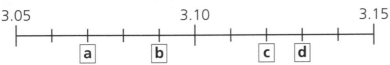

7 Put these numbers in order from smallest to largest.

    0.45   0.78   0.29   0.63   0.12   0.37

Challenge yourself

8 Put these numbers in order from smallest to largest.

    3.13   3.35   1.33   3.15   33.51   1.53

9 Peter has £34.52 and Javid has £35.42.
Who has the most money?

10 Karim has three cards with digits on them. Use each one **once** to complete the number sentences below.

    a) 67.43 > 67.4☐

    b) 32.☐5 < 32.25

    c) 45.☐7 > 45.27

11 Which statements are true about the number 34.67?

    a) It has 60 tenths.   **b)** It has 60 hundredths.   **c)** It has 7 hundredths.

How did you do?

Common decimal equivalents

We need to know the decimal equivalents for some common fractions.

Think of a metre stick.
It shows 100 cm or 1 m

$$0 \qquad \frac{1}{4} \qquad \frac{1}{2} \qquad \frac{3}{4} \qquad 1$$

Half of the metre stick is 50 cm = $\frac{50}{100}$ = 0.5 m = $\frac{1}{2}$

One-quarter of the metre stick is 25 cm = $\frac{25}{100}$ = 0.25 = $\frac{1}{4}$

Three-quarters of the metre stick = 75 cm = $\frac{75}{100}$ = 0.75 = $\frac{3}{4}$

We can show these decimal fractions on our number line.

$$0 \qquad \frac{1}{4} \qquad \frac{1}{2} \qquad \frac{3}{4} \qquad 1$$

$$\qquad \mathbf{0.25} \qquad \mathbf{0.50} \qquad \mathbf{0.75}$$

Warm up

1 Write these decimals as fractions.

   a) 0.5

   b) 0.75

   c) 0.25

2 Write these fractions as decimals.

   a) $\frac{3}{4}$

   b) $\frac{1}{4}$

   c) $\frac{1}{2}$

3 Match these decimals and fractions. One has been done for you.

0.01 $\frac{3}{4}$

$\frac{5}{10}$ 0.25

0.75   0.05

$\frac{1}{4}$ $\frac{1}{100}$

$\frac{5}{100}$ 0.5

4 Jaina makes a jug of squash for the party. Her mum pours half of it into cups. What decimal fraction of squash is left in the jug?

5 Leo's dog is 1 m tall. Sasha's dog is $\frac{3}{4}$ of the height of Leo's dog. How tall is Sasha's dog in m? Give your answer as a decimal.

6 Peter cuts an apple into quarters. He gives one piece away. What decimal fraction has he given away?

7 Find the decimal equivalents of these fractions. Write them in order from smallest to largest.

$\frac{3}{4}$ $\frac{5}{100}$ $\frac{1}{10}$ $\frac{1}{4}$ $\frac{5}{10}$

How did you do?

Fraction problems

1. Which shapes have $\frac{1}{3}$ shaded?

A   **B**   **C**   **D**

2. Copy this shape carefully. Shade $\frac{1}{3}$ of it.

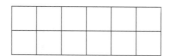

3. Copy and complete the equivalent fractions.

a) $\frac{1}{3} = \frac{?}{12}$

b) $\frac{1}{4} = \frac{2}{?}$

c) $\frac{2}{5} = \frac{?}{10}$

4. Copy these tennis balls. Count them carefully. Draw a circle round $\frac{5}{8}$ of them. How many balls are in your circle?

5. Copy and complete this number sentence, simplifying your answer.

$\frac{2}{9} + \frac{4}{9} =$

Test yourself

6. Write a fraction that is greater than $\frac{1}{4}$ but smaller than $\frac{1}{2}$.

7. Copy and match these fractions to the correct answer.

$\frac{1}{3}$ of 150 is   30

$\frac{1}{2}$ of 90 is   40

$\frac{1}{5}$ of 150 is   45

$\frac{1}{4}$ of 160 is   50

8 Copy and complete these calculations.

a) $\frac{5}{9} + \frac{3}{9} =$

b) $\frac{8}{12} - \frac{5}{12} =$

c) $\frac{8}{16} + \frac{5}{16} =$

d) $\frac{14}{15} - \frac{8}{15} =$

9 What is $\frac{5}{6}$ of 90?

10 Copy and complete this number sentence.

$\frac{6}{\boxed{?}} = \frac{3}{7} = \frac{\boxed{?}}{35}$

11 $\frac{3}{4}$ of my number is 18. What is my number?

12 Leila has a box of 25 coloured beads. 10 of the beads are blue. 5 of the beads are red. The rest of the beads are yellow.

a) What fraction of the beads is red?

b) What fraction of the beads is blue?

c) What fraction of the beads is yellow?

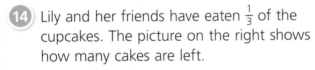

13 Find $\frac{1}{4}$ of £12 and 40 pence.

14 Lily and her friends have eaten $\frac{1}{3}$ of the cupcakes. The picture on the right shows how many cakes are left.

How many cakes were there to start with?

15 Jack has 2 pizzas. He eats $\frac{3}{5}$ of one and his friend Ethan eats $\frac{4}{5}$ of the other one. How much pizza do the boys have left over altogether?

How did you do?

Decimal problems

1 Copy and complete these sequences.

a) 0.56   0.57   0.58   _____   _____   _____

b) 0.83   0.82   0.81   _____   _____   _____

c) 0.18   0.19   _____   0.21   _____   _____

2 Find $\frac{1}{10}$ of these amounts. Give your answer as a decimal.

a) 2   b) 36   c) 18

3 Round these decimals to the nearest whole number.

a) 76.2   b) 19.9   c) 37.8

4 Write the fraction of each shape that is shaded. Give your answer as a decimal. The first one has been done for you.

a)  = 0.3   b)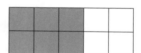

c)    d)

e)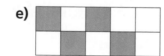

5 Write the decimals that are equivalent to these fractions.

a) $\frac{7}{100}$ b) $\frac{1}{4}$ c) $\frac{2}{10}$

6 Write the decimals at **a**, **b**, **c** and **d**.

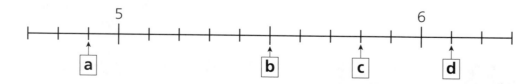

7 Write the decimals that are equivalent to these fractions. The first one has been done for you.

a) $\frac{3}{10}$ = 0.3

b) $\frac{9}{100}$

c) $\frac{7}{10}$

d) $\frac{26}{100}$

e) $\frac{3}{100}$

8 Write the fractions that are equivalent to these decimals. The first one has been done for you.

a) 0.03 = $\frac{3}{100}$

b) 0.02

c) 0.9

d) 0.34

e) 0.75

9 Copy this brick wall and shade 0.75 of it.

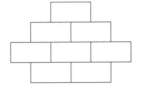

10 Match these decimals and fractions.

$\frac{6}{100}$ 0.7

0.75   0.09

$\frac{7}{10}$ $\frac{3}{4}$

$\frac{9}{100}$ 0.06

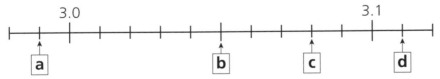

Challenge yourself

11 Write these decimals in order from the smallest to the biggest.

a) 2.6   3.2   6.2   0.6   2.3

b) 14.60   41.61   14.26   14.62

12 Find $\frac{1}{100}$ of these amounts. Give your answer as a decimal.

a) 45   b) 16   c) 3

13 Write the decimals at **a**, **b**, **c** and **d**.

3.0   3.1

a   **b**   **c**   **d**

14 Mirah has a collection of 40 soft toys. $\frac{1}{10}$ of her toys are teddy bears. How many teddy bears does Mirah have? Give your answer as a decimal.

15 Becky's mum bakes some fudge. She cuts the fudge into 20 pieces. She gives Becky 0.25 of the tray. How many pieces of fudge does Becky have?

How did you do?

Progress test 5

1. Write the larger decimal from each pair.

   a) 3.45   3.54

   b) 0.03   0.30

   c) 7.32   7.23

2. Copy and complete the matching pairs. The first one has been done for you.

   a) $1.00 = \frac{1}{1}$

   b) $0.25 =$

   c) $\quad = \frac{1}{2}$

   d) $0.75 =$

3. Put these amounts in order from the smallest to the largest.

   £0.43   £4.53   £0.34   £3.45   £0.04

4. Round these decimals to one decimal place.

   a) 3.4

   b) 76.7

   c) 14.9

5. Convert these amounts to pence.

   a) £0.32

   b) £1.65

   c) £0.05

6. Put these fractions and decimals in order from the smallest to the largest.

   0.90 $\frac{1}{2}$ 0.25 $\frac{3}{4}$ 0.10

7. Divide by 100 to convert these cm to m.

   a) 45 cm

   b) 50 cm

   c) 93 cm

8. Leila thinks of a decimal number. She rounds it to the nearest whole number and gets the answer 5. What number could Leila have been thinking of?

9. Rasmig pours 2 litres of squash into a jug. Emily pours $\frac{1}{10}$ of it into a cup. How much is in Emily's cup? Give your answer in litres.

10. Round these decimals to the nearest whole number.

    a) 7.6

    b) 32.2

    c) 176.8

    d) 99.9

Score ◯ / 10

1 Round these decimals to the nearest whole number.

a) 6.3

b) 5.8

c) 2.9

2 Round these decimals to one decimal place.

a) 4.59

b) 7.26

c) 8.71

3 Put these decimals in order from smallest to largest.

3.7   7.3   3.9   3.4   7.5

4 Put these amounts in order from smallest to largest.

£2.45   £4.20   £5.42   £4.25   £2.54

5 Copy and match the fractions with their decimal equivalents.

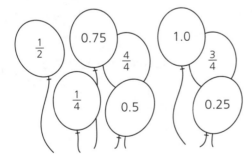

6 What is $\frac{1}{2}$ of £3?

7 What is $\frac{1}{4}$ of 6 metres?

8 Draw a line to match the equivalent measures.

0.75 m   75 cm

0.7 kg   0.75 km

750 m   700 g

9 Divide by 100 to put these measurements in order from smallest to largest.

35 cm   0.3 m   300 cm   350 cm   0.33 cm

10 Put these amounts in order from smallest to largest.

50p   £1.25   £0.52   152p   25p

Score ⬤ / 10

Mixed test

1 Look at these fractions. Find three pairs which are equivalent.

$\frac{8}{12}$ $\quad$ $\frac{9}{12}$ $\quad$ $1\frac{2}{10}$ $\quad$ $\frac{3}{4}$ $\quad$ $\frac{2}{3}$ $\quad$ $1\frac{1}{5}$

2 Write **true** or **false** for each statement.

a) $\frac{3}{5} < \frac{1}{4}$

b) $\frac{4}{7} = \frac{12}{21}$

c) $\frac{5}{10} < \frac{4}{5}$

3 Anna has two digit cards. One of the cards is a 4. Write both the fractions that Anna can make with her cards that equal $\frac{1}{2}$. Use the 4 once as the numerator and once as the denominator.

4 Write these fractions in order from smallest to largest.

$\frac{7}{100}$ $\quad$ $\frac{70}{100}$ $\quad$ 0.25 $\quad$ $\frac{3}{4}$ $\quad$ 0.02

5 The long-distance running course is 23 km long. Nina practises by running $\frac{1}{100}$ of the distance every day. How far does Nina run each day? Give your answer in km.

6 The paddling pool holds 96 litres of water. Naga uses $\frac{1}{100}$ of the water in the pool to water her plants. How much water does Naga scoop out? Give your answer in litres.

7 Jo has collected 96 football cards. She gives $\frac{2}{3}$ of them to her brother. How many cards does she give away?

8 Look at these fractions. Which two fractions are greater than $\frac{1}{2}$?

$\frac{3}{6}$ $\quad$ $\frac{4}{5}$ $\quad$ $\frac{2}{6}$ $\quad$ $\frac{4}{8}$ $\quad$ $\frac{2}{3}$

9 Leo paints a wall that is 3 m long. His sister helps by painting $\frac{1}{10}$ of it. How much of the wall does his sister paint? Give your answer in metres.

10 Jerome has a bag with 7 red and 8 blue marbles in it.

a) What fraction of each colour is in the bag?

b) Jerome adds another two blue marbles. How many marbles are there in the bag now?

c) What fraction is blue?

11 Peter has $\frac{9}{12}$ of a pizza. He eats $\frac{4}{12}$. How much pizza does he have left?

12 Miriam has 88 metres of ribbon. She cuts it into 100 equal pieces. How long is each piece? Give your answer in metres.

13 Lena runs 3.67 km, Millie runs 3760 m. Who runs the furthest distance?

14 Round 3.8 to the nearest whole number.

15 Jaina saves £12.80. She spends $\frac{1}{4}$ of her savings. How much does Jaina spend?

16 Farmer Bill has 32 chickens. $\frac{1}{4}$ of his chickens are brown. How many brown chickens does Farmer Bill have?

17 Leo has 25 metres of rope. He cuts it into 10 equal lengths. How long is each piece?

18 Sunni walks $\frac{1}{4}$ of 1 kilometre. How far does Sunni walk?

19 The girls are baking flapjack. Freya weighs out 270 g of sugar, Mina weighs out 0.25 kg of oats. Who has the biggest amount of baking ingredients?

20 Manish is running every day in training for the cross-country event. Put his distances in order from the smallest to largest.

3.45 km   5.34 km   5.43 km
3.54 km   4.53 km

Published by Keen Kite Books
An imprint of HarperCollins*Publishers*
The News Building, 1 London Bridge Street
London SE1 9GF

ISBN 9780008161880

Text © 2015 Frances Naismith

Design © 2015 Keen Kite Books, an imprint of
HarperCollins*Publishers* Ltd